The m&m's® BRAND

Color Pattern Book

Barbara Barbieri McGrath
Illustrated by Roger Glass

ihi Charlesbridge

Special thanks to Will M., Lynn S., Mary Ann S., Dominic B., and Susan S.—BBM

Published by Charlesbridge Publishing
85 Main Street, Watertown, MA 02472
(617) 926-0329
www.charlesbridge.com

Library of Congress Cataloging-in-Publication Data
McGrath, Barbara Barbieri, 1954 —
    The "M&M'S"® brand color pattern book / Barbara Barbieri McGrath;
illustrated by Roger Glass.
    p.cm.
    Summary: Rhyming text describes how to sort "M&M'S"® to make vari-
ous color patterns.
    ISBN 1-57091-416-8 (reinforced for library use)
    ISBN 1-57091-417-6 (softcover)
1. Colors—Juvenile literature. 2. Sequences (Mathematics)—Juvenile literature.
[1. Color.] I. Glass, Roger, ill. II Title.

QC495.5.M3767 2002
535.6—dc21   2001028997

Printed in the United States of America
(hc) 10 9 8 7 6 5 4 3 2 1
(sc) 10 9 8 7 6 5 4 3 2 1

The illustrations in this book were done in Macromedia Freehand.
The display type and text type were set in Helvetica and Times.
Color separations were made by Phoenix Color, Rockaway, New Jersey
Printed and bound by Phoenix Color, Rockaway, New Jersey
Production supervision by Brian G. Walker
Designed by Roger Glass

**With love to Lindsay B.
—B.B.M.**

**With love to Dee Ann, Jenny, and Laura
—R.G.**

Open a package.
Pour out every candy.
To make color patterns,
"M&M'S"® come in handy.

Count all the colors. Can you find six?
Let's make some order out of this mix.

1 2 3 4 5 6

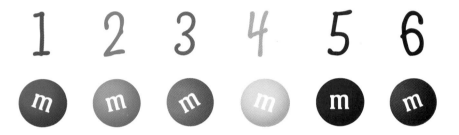

First sort the red, orange, and blue.
Then group the yellow, green, and brown, too.

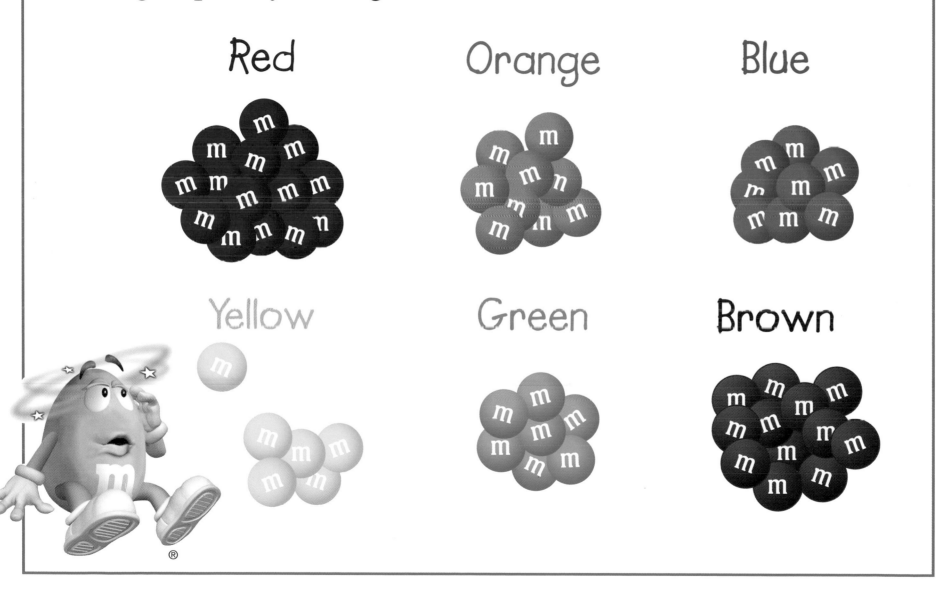

Red

Orange

Blue

Yellow

Green

Brown

To make the first pattern, there are two colors to choose.
Put a red, then a yellow until there's none left to use.

Now we'll just add green to this long candy line.
Red, yellow, then green. You're doing just fine.

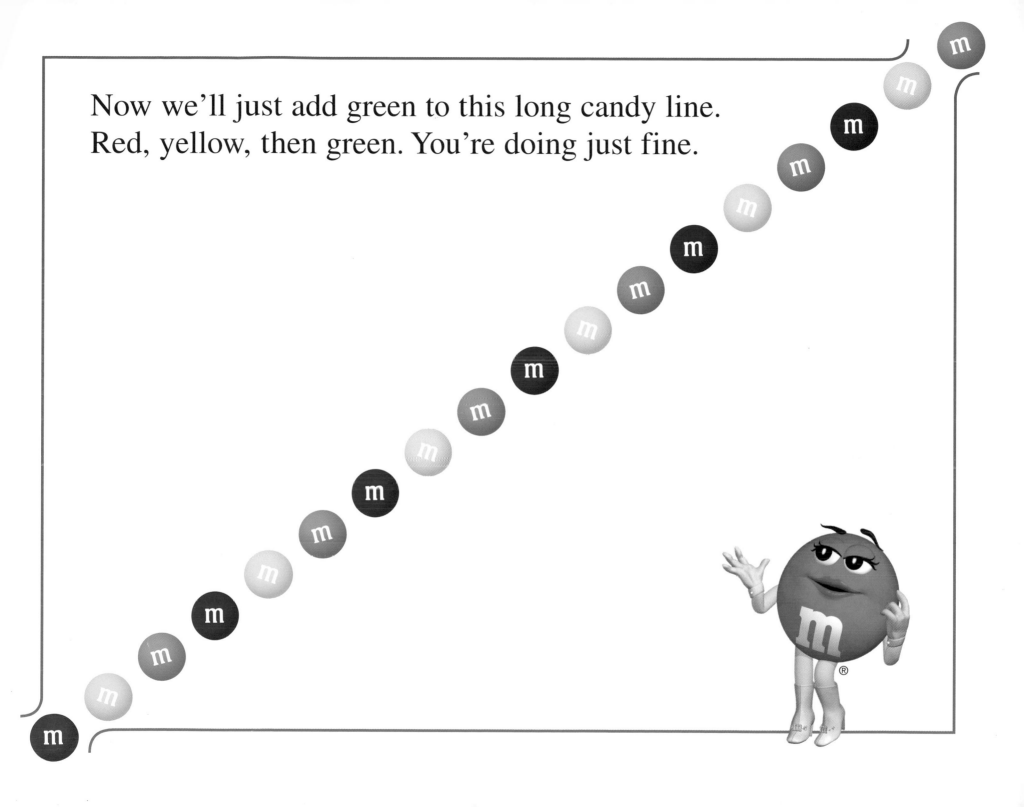

Can you make all the blue, brown, and orange fit?
Red, yellow, green, blue, brown, orange—
that's it!

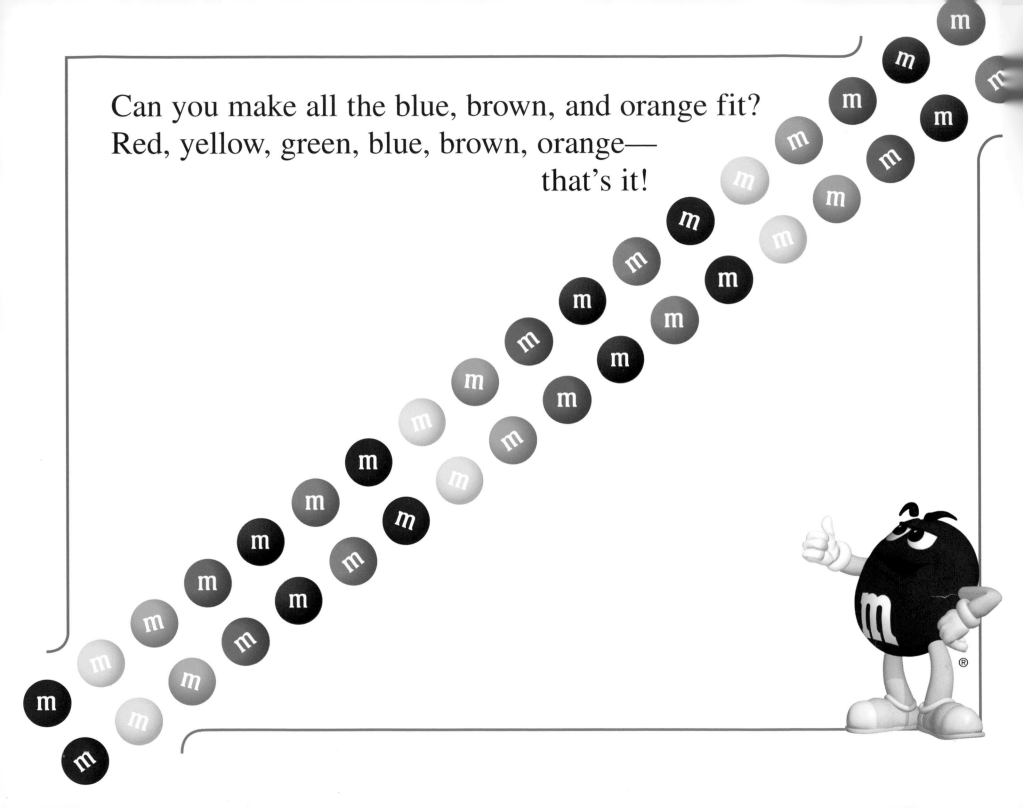

Let's say the colors. They're all in sight.
Start from the left, and read to the right.

Red! Yellow! Green!

Blue! Brown! Orange!

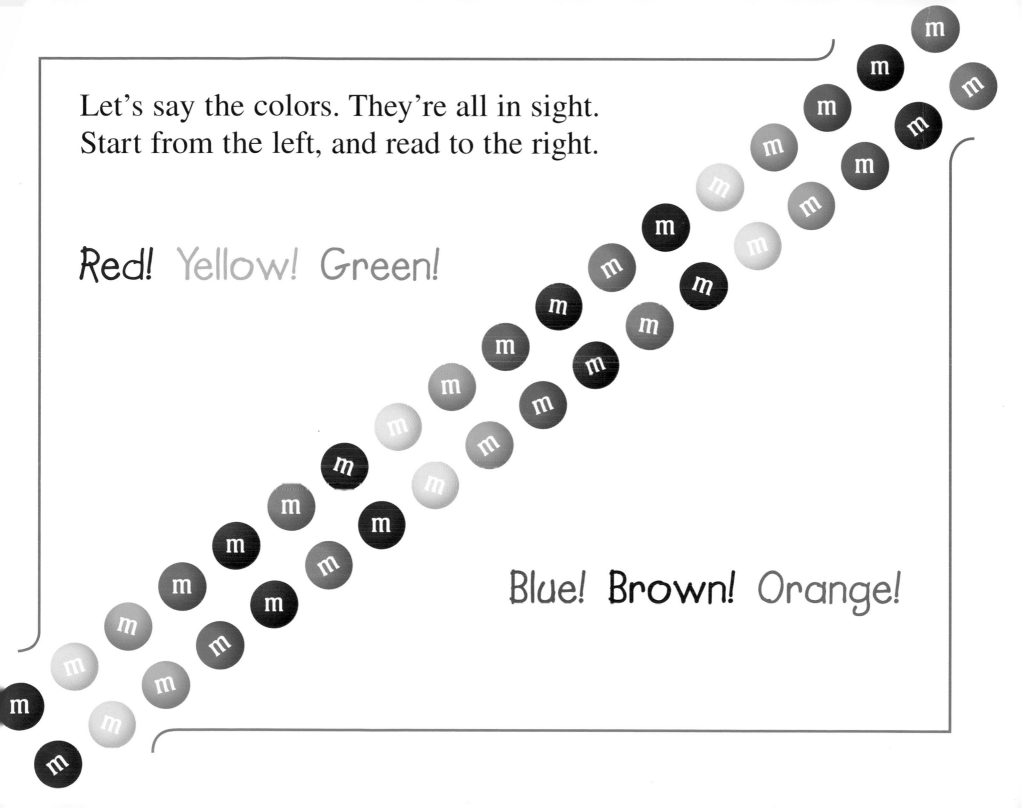

Take that six-color pattern in order, and then—
Repeat the order, again, again, and again.

What's fun about patterns
Is they always repeat.
Are there any extras?
Those you may eat!

Arrange four of each color—here's something more...
When added together, you'll find twenty-four.

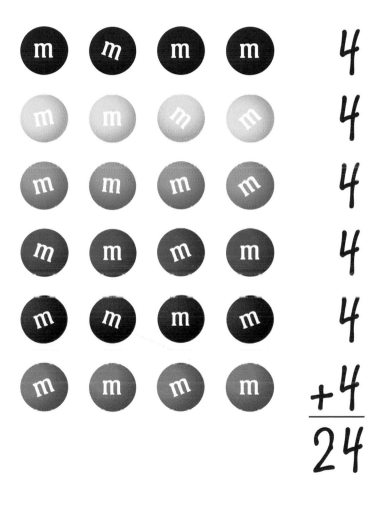

$$
\begin{array}{r}
4 \\
4 \\
4 \\
4 \\
4 \\
+4 \\
\hline
24
\end{array}
$$

Now try this pattern. It's easy to do.
Red, red, blue. Then red, red, blue.

Start a new pattern on the next line down.
Yellow, yellow, brown. Then yellow, yellow, brown.

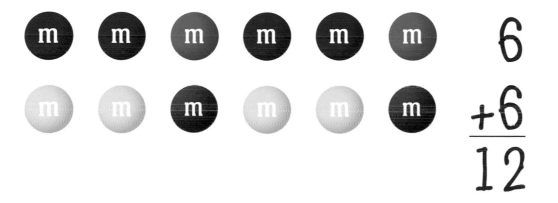

$$6$$
$$+6$$
$$\overline{12}$$

That's twelve! Plus six more is eighteen.
Orange, orange green. Then orange, orange, green.

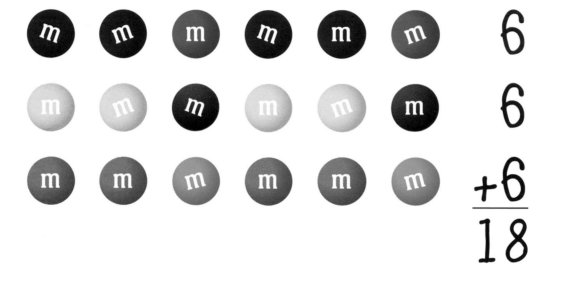

6
6
+6
18

Make a big circle. Try to fit them all in.
Now find three places where the patterns begin!

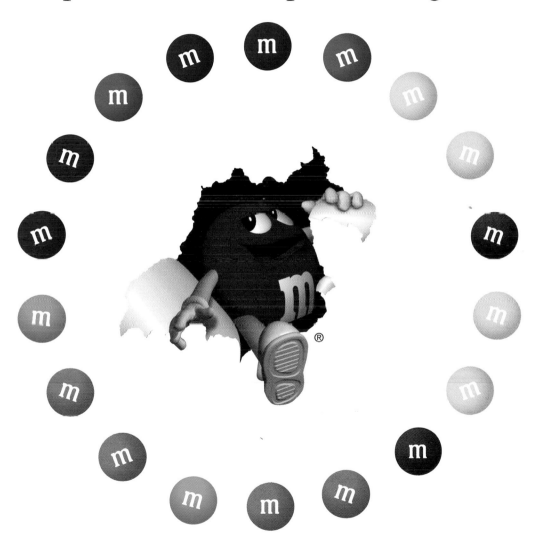

Six candies left over. Here's a fun thing to do:
Eat an "M&M'S"® pattern. Green, brown, blue.
Green, brown, blue.

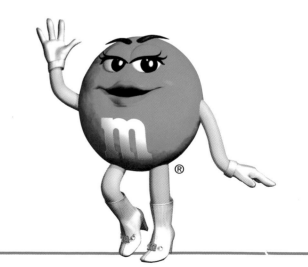

With the new color patterns that you can now see,
Ask a grown-up to show you…six times three!

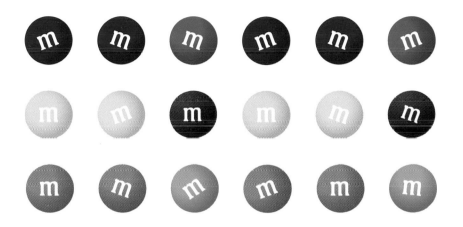

6x3=18

Eat the two M&M'S® that are first in each row.
Two red, two yellow, two orange—down they go!

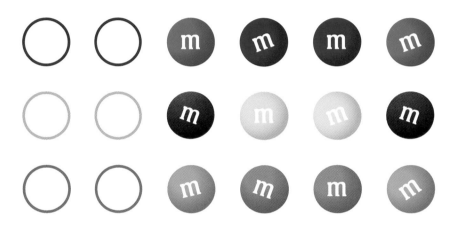

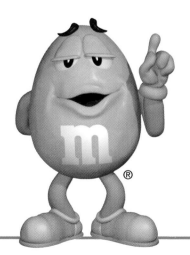

Look up, look down, and by moving just three,
Patterns appear! (I think you'll agree.)

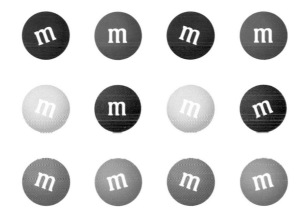

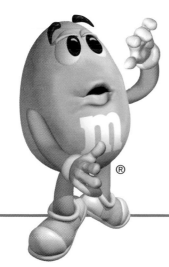

Let's make a pattern that is totally new.
Place all the candies by color, by two.

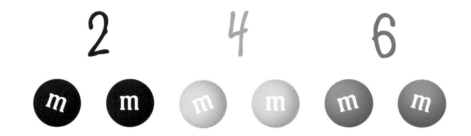

8 10 12

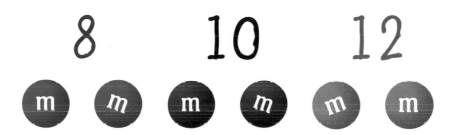

Can you count by twos, by color? Just try.
Two, four, six, eight, ten, twelve...oh my!

Put them like this
and learn a fun way to count.

Skip count by two
to get the total amount.

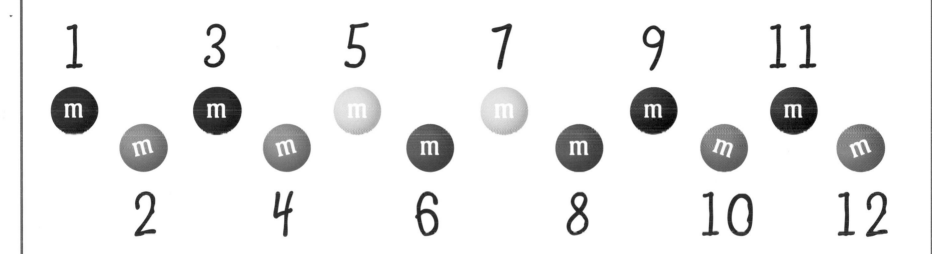

1   3   5   7   9   11

2   4   6   8   10   12

Do you see what I see?
If you do, give a nod…
Bottom numbers are even,
the top ones are odd!

Design your own pattern
For this page in the book.

Try again! Use all the colors.

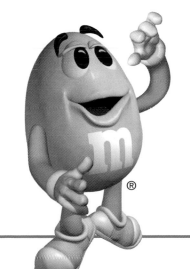

How do they look?

Are any of your patterns the same as these?

Try again! Use all the colors.

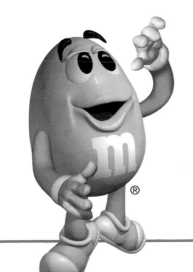

How do they look?

Are any of your patterns the same as these?

Follow this pattern,
if you please.

Eat one of each color. See what you've done?

Now, for each of six colors, you have only one.

Orange, blue, brown, yellow, green, red—
no need to wait...

Use six that are left
to celebrate!

This final page is called a review.
It shows the new tasks you've learned to do.

Sorting by color

Skip counting

1		3		5		7		9		11	

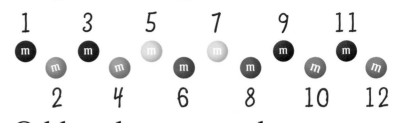

| | 2 | | 4 | | 6 | | 8 | | 10 | | 12 |

Odd and even numbers

6 Color patterns

Identifying patterns

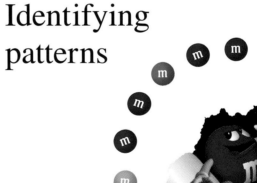

12 Color patterns

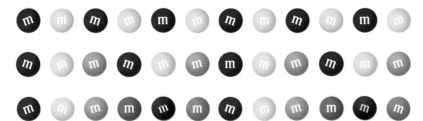